DEM●S

Demos is an independent think tank committed to radical thinking on the long-term problems facing the UK and other advanced industrial societies.

It aims to develop ideas – both theoretical and practical – to help shape the politics of the twenty first century, and to improve the breadth and quality of political debate.

Demos publishes books and a regular journal and undertakes substantial empirical and policy oriented research projects. Demos is a registered charity.

In all its work Demos brings together people from a wide range of backgrounds in business, academia, government, the voluntary sector and the media to share and cross-fertilise ideas and experiences.

For further information and
subscription details please contact:
Demos
The Mezzanine
Elizabeth House
39 York Road
London SE1 7NQ
email: mail@demos.co.uk
www.demos.co.uk

Basildon

The mood of the nation

Dennis Hayes and
Alan Hudson

First published in 2001 by
Demos
The Mezzanine
Elizabeth House
39 York Road
London SE1 7NQ

ISBN 1 84180 060 0
Printed in Great Britain
Design by Lindsay Nash

Contents

Acknowledgements

We would like to thank the following: Tom Bentley, Benn Jupp, Gavin Poynter and participants at a Demos seminar for their comments. Our thanks also go to our research assistants: Caroline Dobbs, Pam Dunnill, Robert Fletcher, Michael Joslin, Patrick Hayes, Gemma Hills, Anna Rischel and Neil White, and to Con O'Brien for political background. We are grateful to officers of Basildon Council for their help and advice, in particular, Mark Gaynor, Paul Montford, Helen Newport, John Robb, Tom Gardiner and Ray Stephenson, and to Dudley Webster from Basildon College. But above all, our thanks go to Alf Dove MBE, Tracey Clark and the people of Basildon.

Preface

This book is based upon interviews with 500 skilled workers (employed, recently unemployed, retired or their spouses) carried out in Basildon during the summer following the general election of 1997 and subsequent discussions with local policy makers, focus groups and individuals. It draws upon a previous survey by the same researchers of a similar group of five hundred skilled workers carried out in Basildon during the summer following the general election of 1992. We began in that year with what we thought was a one-off visit to see if there was any empirical evidence to support the sociological claims being made about the existence of a 'new working class' that had adopted Thatcherite values. We returned to Basildon to review our original conclusions and to broaden the survey. Our original focus and concerns had been narrowly political. In the intervening five years they seemed to us strangely outdated. In a post political period we had to ask a different set of questions to enable us to understand what people really thought.

Our findings will be surprising and challenging to many people. Academics and researchers will find that they will overturn some cherished and fashionable sociological theories. Journalists and other opinion formers will find that the views of many commentators about what ordinary people think are nothing but groundless prejudices. For employers, managers and trade unionists they will provide both good and bad news. National and local policy makers will find here an articulation of the problem of how to connect with their constituencies. More importantly, we also hope that ordinary people, not least the people of Basildon, will find in this short work a reflection of themselves.

What is presented here is part of a longitudinal study of the changing nature of the working class from the post-cold war decade into the twenty-first century. We will return to Basildon after the 2001 general election to undertake another survey.

1. Introduction

At 11.22pm on Thursday 9 April 1992, Basildon achieved its fifteen minutes of political fame. The re-election of David Amess, a Thatcherite Conservative, was heralded by the pundits as definitive confirmation of Labour's worst secret fears. The country had, yet again, rejected them, and they would have to spend five more years in opposition.

Since then, the landscape of British politics has changed dramatically, but Basildon is still afforded special significance. It is a barometer for the mood of the nation: swift to declare on election night, it is Middle England territory, a town dominated by skilled manual workers, the 'C2s' whose habits, values and preferences are believed by both left and right to hold the key to electoral success.

Basildon has returned general election results in line with the national trend at every election since the 1950s. This does not mean that they always elected a candidate from the party which formed a government. Exceptionally in 1964 Edward Gardner QC held his seat for the Tories, reflecting the fragility of the Wilson government's hold on power. Eric Moonman won in 1966 with a narrow majority of 1,642. He lost to the Tories in 1970, only to take the seat again in 1974 with a huge majority.[1]

Throughout the 1980s, Basildon's reputation hardened as a laboratory of the Thatcher revolution. In 1992 the pundits started to ask whether Labour could ever hope to win over such places, proselytisers for the property-owning democracy, the classless society and freedom from the Nanny State.

The 1992 defeat catalysed the creation of 'New Labour', a social-democratic party with popular appeal. When Angela Smith won Basildon for

New Labour at 49 minutes past midnight on 2 May 1997, with a swing of 14.7 per cent, this result was also awarded deep political significance.

Four years on, and with another general election looming, what has happened to hearts and minds in Basildon? This study retraces the political journey of Basildon's people to discover what motivates them, how fast their political allegiances hold, and how they measure their own aspirations and identities against what politics has to offer.

We found an overall picture which we believe is representative of large parts of the UK, and which presents severe challenges for political parties and government:

● Basildonians attribute the successes and quality of their own lives to their own efforts.
● At the same time they expect life to become more difficult for the next generation and believe that life in Britain is getting worse.
● They believe that despite their own best efforts they cannot make a difference to the big picture.
● They want government to spend less on itself, more on the provision of services but without interfering in their lives.
● They have less allegiance to all political parties than before and no discernible identification with other institutions such as the church, monarchy or trade unions.
● They do not belong to very much; even sports clubs do not figure greatly in their lives.
● Their identifications are local, familial and cultural : the family is the most important resource and network, Basildon is a good enough place to live, and being working class is a worthy badge.
● Education is the cutting edge of the ongoing Basildonian search to better yourself.

Our report is based on interviews with 500 skilled workers carried out in Basildon during the summer of 1997, shortly after New Labour's landslide victory. We subsequently undertook discussions with local policymakers, focus groups and individuals. We have also drawn upon a previous survey of a similar group of 500 skilled workers in Basildon during the summer of 1992, shortly after John Major's election victory.[2]

The experience and attitudes of the skilled working class are central to the discussion of the Basildon phenomenon. Even though it is constantly changing, Basildon remains an overwhelmingly skilled working-class town. The sons and daughters of engineering workers are now much more likely to be in financial services and computer software. These changes are representative of more general shifts in British life.

Basildon was the seventh and largest of the post-war New Towns planned for outer London. Its first wave of inhabitants felt themselves to be at the forefront of the hopes and challenges involved in the reconstruction of post-war Britain. Their 'frontier' mentality has influenced the outlooks and aspirations of subsequent generations of Basildonians, in ways that now pose difficult challenges for politicians and policy-makers.

A good example is the strong sense of individualism and self-improvement. This outlook predated Thatcherism, but became bound up with the ideological notions of possessive individualism that emerged in the 1980s. During those years Basildonians certainly became property-owners, but in accordance with desires that stretched back to the post-war slum clearance and relocation programmes rather than any fulfilment of a radical Conservative mission. Today the drive for self-improvement manifests itself in a widespread, vague and for politicians, unsettling desire for greater educational opportunities. It is unsettling because the desires of Basildonians seem to defy New Labour policy priorities.

We found another phenomenon emerging strongly in Basildon: a profound detachment from all forms of collective political process or social agency. Local people are living their lives increasingly in the private sphere, especially through family life. They care little for public forums, they do not join in public activities, they have little faith in local decision-makers. Again, this should ring alarm bells with politicians, for it is a sure sign that the legitimacy of key political forms is on the wane.

Local policy-makers are alive to this problem, but they cannot solve it alone. Besides, it is not theirs alone to solve: our argument is that the people of this town reveal much about changing attitudes the length and breadth of Britain. Long after the pollsters have given up trying to predict our reactions to every subtle act of triangulation by spin-obsessed political parties, there will still be a need for democrats to puzzle over how to recreate and renew the civic and political institutions that are the backbone of a thousand towns like Basildon. We hope our findings help.

2. Why Basildon?

During the 1980s Basildon acquired doubtful celebrity status. Its residents were dubbed 'Basildon Man' and 'Essex Girl'; the essential qualities of each caricature were subjected to intense scrutiny and mockery. Basildon Man was a shell-suited, tasteless, XRi-driving twenty-something bloke, easily recognisable in the fictional TV character 'Loadsamoney'.

Loadsamoney was the deeply unpleasant creation of the Labour-supporting comedian Harry Enfield. But in December 1992 the then Tory minister, Stephen Norris, employed the same picture when he characterised Essex Man as having 'a great deal of money and very little taste'.[3] Basildon Man may have been a Tory voter, but you wouldn't want him in the golf club. Essex Girl was a sexually predatory twenty-something female with short skirts, large hoop earrings and a pronounced estuary accent.

These crude lifestyle caricatures were an implausible attempt to define a new group of workers with a new Thatcherite ideology to match. Basildon's working class were not recognisable as traditional cloth-capped, pigeon-fancying, horny handed sons of toil. But neither was this a morally degenerate, feckless but ultimately pitiable 'underclass'. To conventional politicians of both right and left, these workers seemed brash, aggressive and threatening.

The stereotype became further confused with that other famous Eighties phenomenon, the yuppie finance broker. Yet, despite apocryphal stories of colonies of Rolls-Royce owners, Basildon Man was not surfing the wave of City speculation. In our 1992 survey of skilled workers we found that two-thirds (64 per cent) of our respondents earned less than £15,000.[4] Basildon's workers were no better off than their fellow workers elsewhere; in fact, they were relatively poor by the standards of the South East.

Our 1997 survey found that 60 per cent earned less than £15,000. If we take inflation into account and the fact that the working population of Basildon is, on average, slightly older than it was in 1992, then real earnings have probably gone down. Thirty-two per cent of the 1997 sample earned less than £10,000, the regional average wage at that time. New industries and service sector jobs have not brought loadsamoney to Basildon.

Despite the caricatures, Basildon is a particularly interesting place.

Basildon has a higher proportion of skilled workers (C2s) than any other town in Britain. It retains a light manufacturing base, with 45 per cent of its jobs in manufacturing and transport. Service industry employment, currently at 33 per cent of jobs, is increasing, but skilled manual work still accounts for more than a third of the workforce.[5]

The people of Basildon seem to share an unusually strong sense of aspiration. Their desire to achieve was evident from the early days of the town, portrayed in the emblem of the first residents' association –

Figure 1. The truth about Basildon Man		
Media Image	*Reality 1992*	*Reality 1997*
Tasteless: shell suits for men, short skirts and large 'hoop' earrings for women	Some truth in this choice of clothes but it is based on relatively low earnings	Ordinary or smart dress
Loads of money	64 % less than £15,000 pa	60 per cent earning less than £15,000. Relatively poor
Conservative	Yes. That is, they voted Conservative, but 24% rejected all Conservative policies	No. They voted New Labour and 39% rejected all Conservative policies. They are increasingly disengaged from politics.
Classless	75% describe themselves as working class	73% describe themselves as working class

a pioneer wagon – and is echoed is the drive toward self- improvement that we discovered in today's young Basildonians.

There is a historical explanation for this character. Basildon was the largest and the last of Britain's seven post-war new towns. Its first wave of residents may have been moved there in a pragmatic wave of slum clearance but mostly they made the choice to move. They were not just displaced by the Blitz, but were actively seeking a new life. This made them different from their contemporaries who remained in East Ham and Dagenham and from skilled workers in similar northern towns. Basildonians are alive to the notion that their new town harbours a new population 'on the move'. Many we interviewed stressed that they wanted to 'get on'.

As Eric Moonman, Basildon's longest serving Labour MP, put it: 'People who came thought there was something to aspire to in Basildon. They could do more, better and faster. *It was like a little bit of America in Essex.*'[6]

One indicator of this aspirational bent is the town's rapid shift to home ownership, which rose from 53 per cent in 1981 to 71 per cent in 1996. The search for a home of their own was central to the hopes of first-generation Basildonians. A different definition of home owner-ship was at the heart of the shift in political allegiance of a later gener-ation. Today, while there is still concern for home security, education has become the medium through which people aspire to enhanced life opportunities. Among our 1997 survey respondents, 52 per cent believed education and training was the best way to get on. Tracey Clark is a good example:

'If you don't have ambition you can't do anything. Education usually backs you up a lot. I want to get on. My sister's the same as me: she's ambitious.

'Jobs are getting harder, education's getting harder. Young people have got advantages, like growing up with computers. They've got disadvantages in other ways – in getting a job. They are going to find it really hard. They're going to be pushed so much to get an education.'

Portrait 1

Alf Dove is a Basildon pioneer, representative of the postwar community that has disappeared.

Pioneering Days

Alf was an East Ender, born in Shoreditch on 8 February 1919. After being away six years during the Second World War, he went to live in Dagenham. In 1952 he literally got on his bike and cycled to Basildon to become the manager of the new Co-op, bringing his family with him to live over the store. It was an exciting time:

'Suddenly, the chance of starting a new life. …The concept of the new town was, you came here from the smoke and you got a house. People like me just back from the war I was pleased just to have a house to rent. So our ambition was: If only we could get a place to rent! And it came along. If you worked in a factory you rented a house. Marvellous. A garden. Flowers. Everyone was happy!

Alf eventually got a new house in The Fryth that remains his home to the present day. He describes that time as 'real pioneer stuff'. The new tenants' logo was a covered waggon.

'We often went back. We had the new town blues. We even called a psychiatrist in from Runwell. And we said, look – why are people going back?. He said, Well, that's easy: they want to go back to their mum!. There were good early days because we were together. Community spirit and everything.'

Involved in the formation of tenants' associations, Alf was in the Labour Party and an active trade unionist. *'We, the people, were trade unionists!'*, he declares with passion.

Building Basildon

'I can tell you exactly when it stopped and how we evolved into Basildon Man…. Gradually more industry came. Wives were getting jobs. Up till then one man had his job and that was it — mainly building operatives because the first lot who were here built the town. Then we got Carreras [cigarette makers] and everybody started to get richer. Then we got the bangers. Someone had been to Carreras and saved their money up, a couple of hundred quid bought a banger. Everybody had a banger. Everybody had their engines out on the streets. And that's what started it. The getting together, the keeping together started to go. You can't turn a working-class guy into middle class, but you can't blame them for having ambitions.

Alf was elected to the council in 1956 and was the first New Town tenant to become Chair of the council in 1963. Through the first year of his office he attended functions on his scooter, until he was given a civic car in 1964. Interviewed in 1991 by a local journalist for a book to celebrate the fortieth anniversary of the town, he talked of people having to make their own amusements and struggling to bring up their children and pay the rent. Nevertheless, he would live nowhere else.

'New Towns were different. They had better standards of housing for ordinary working-class people. There were homes with central heating and bathrooms. For most it was heaven'[7]

'From errand boy to shop manager, from tenant's treasurer to council chairman....that's Alf Dove's route to fame. He likes natty hats, eating well, people in general, gardening, modern art and Basildon. He does not own a car – 'can't afford one' – would like to spend more time with his children, to try his hand at oil painting and to see everyone who needs a house getting one'.[8]

The Golden Age: Socialism 1971–79

'Labour was in control from 1971 to 1979 – eight solid years. We had socialism then. The OAPs went on holidays. Bus passes. If they couldn't get out of the house they had a food parcel or a food voucher. A coal subsidy or a heating subsidy. Television subsidy. That was real socialism in those days because we looked after the old first.

'Then we looked at the capital building and we said: Right, every neighbourhood or part of a neighbourhood should have a swimming pool and so on and so on... That's when we embarked on spend, spend, spend, which years later caught up with us.'

The end, when it came, was based on complementary ambitions to those of the pioneering Basildonians:

'Thatcher came in. She killed the unions. She killed any community spirit the unions imbued in the workers. That's what happened. That and the houses. That's when I think the big change came. It was every man for himself. She said: There's no such thing as society.

'Suddenly there was the new urge to be middle class, to own your own property. This is the great change. It was 85 per cent Labour in my ward right up to the mid-eighties. Then, knocking on the door: Going to vote for us this time? Sorry Alf, she gave me my house. They had a mortgage around their necks but, she gave me my house. This is the beginning of Basildon Man, I think. House owner, car owner, keeping up with the Joneses".

Basildon at 50

Alf Dove has lived in Basildon for 47 years. He retired this in May 1999 after 43 years as a councillor. When we interviewed him he had just been to collect his MBE. On the feelings and fears of the town in middle age he is most unhappy about education:

'Why is Basildon so low down in its achievements in education? We're not the only ones like this. At Fryern's School – I was a governor of that for many years it has just closed at the end of the year – 18 per cent got five GCSEs.

continued over

'Even the finest school, over at Woodlands, where there's lots of middle-class people – the figure's 32 per cent: nobody's reached the 47 per cent which is the average. That's why we've had to bring in the education action zone at this end of the town. It's terrible, really.

'Now, whose fault was that? We often ask ourselves because we were in charge of education in the sixties … I happened to be chairman of the council. First thing I started to do was to change the system from secondary modern.... I consulted everybody, the head teachers, the cleaners, the caretakers. The teachers said: Have an all-through school. You give 'em a chance to break at sixteen and they'll leave. So that's what we did. Years afterwards – and this is where it was disappointing – It was supposed to have produced 150 sixth-formers. How many did you think we had? In Fryern's about three.

'I often ask myself what happened. Something went wrong. I could never put my finger on it.

'You can see how our socialism was. It was because of Labour being there from '71 to '79, out from '79 to '82, back again from '82 to '89. In '92 we lost every bloody seat. That's when the Tories took over and all my socialism went out of the window.

About crime and unemployment he is less down-hearted:

It's not unemployment as such, it's the fear of unemployment. Why did I start the Unemployed Workers' Centre? I was deputy leader and my leader said: We've heard about unemployed workers' centres; go and get one. So I did. I got the trade unions together and the corporation built the hut. That was in '82. Then we had 11,000 unemployed. Now it's down to 2,000. It's like crime. The incidence of crime around here is not big crime but it's annoying crime.

He remains positive about the town and the people and about New Labour :

'Marvellous. For eighteen years I'd been knocking at doors, asking: Will you vote Labour?' and was heartily sick of them saying, NO. Now there was this opportunity. I don't care if Tony Blair was a Tory. He was our leader. I said, I'm so fed up with losing.

'I think he's bloody marvellous. I saw him at the recent conference. I said, he's good – like Churchill, only a modern day Churchill. No — it was the Kennedy touch. The moral touch. You've got problems but you've also got responsibilities. It's time we told people this. This is where the council comes into it: it's gradually changing, because they haven't got any money. The golden days of socialism are all gone.

'Did people depend on the council too much? They did, because we deliberately let them do that. Marvellous things for everybody. The seventies. A golden age.'

It is against this strongly developed sense of self-improvement that Basildonians will judge political parties and their policies. That's why Basildon is an important constituency.

It used to be the Labour Party that benefited most from Basildonians' aspirations. Up until the opening of the hospital in 1973, there were many civic campaigns for a better environment and public resources. People's aims were collective and congruent with those of town planners. The history of community and tenants' campaigns verifies this.

By the end of the 1970s, support for Labour had declined. It seemed more plausible to get on under Tory rule, as we found in our 1992 survey.

In 1992 Basildon's skilled workers associated the Labour Party with poverty and welfare, hopelessness and failure. They saw it as the party for losers. Basildonians said they wanted to help themselves rather than wait around for someone else to sort out their lives. Many saw that Labour was a barrier to taking control of their lives and making something of themselves. For a period, through thick and thin, the pronouncements of the Tories had tapped into their aspirations

By 1997 a decade of failure opened the door for New Labour. But as we will see, this electoral shift cannot be taken for granted. It masks a deeper underlying change in people's attitudes to politics, making it harder for any collective institution to claim their allegiance for very long.

3. Understanding Basildonians

How do the residents of Basildon see themselves in terms of class, work, civic life and family? What is most important to them? What changes do they think are happening in their lives and in the wider world?

The responses offer some important insights for politicians of both right and left.

Class

On 7 October 1948, Lewis Silkin, Minister of Town and Country Planning, set out his vision for the town to an audience in Laindon, Basildon:

> 'Basildon will become a city which people from all over the
> world will want to visit, where all classes of the community can
> meet freely together on equal terms and enjoy common cultural
> and recreational facilities. Basildon will not be a place that is
> ugly, grimy and full of paving stones like many large modern
> towns. It will be something which the people deserve; the best
> possible town that modern knowledge, commerce, science and
> civilisation can produce.'[9]

It is commonly asserted that class consciousness has been largely eroded during the past twenty years. Andrew Adonis , an adviser to Tony Blair, wrote in 1997, for instance: 'Many are unsure of their class or reject the idea that they even belong to one'.[10] Adonis concluded: 'The old labels "working-" and "middle-class" make less and less sense in the context of rapidly changing patterns of income, lifestyle and authority'.[11] While

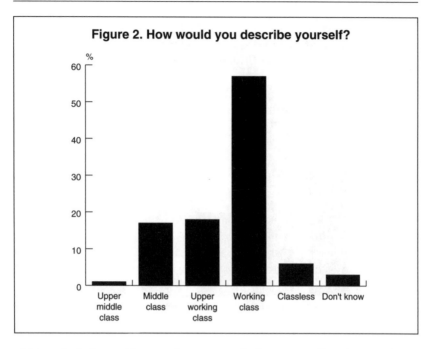

Figure 2. How would you describe yourself?

this analysis has widespread currency, it does not tally with our findings in Basildon.

We found in 1992 that 75 per cent of our survey respondents identified themselves as working class. The figure in 1997 was 73 per cent (Figure 2).

Class is also perceived to have a strong influence on life chances. Basildonians do not buy into the idea that they live in a classless society. Between 1992 and 1997 the sense of grievance and unfairness at class inequality increased significantly.

In 1992, 60 per cent felt that class discrimination was important in determining people's life chances, but by 1997 this had increased to 75 per cent – an opinion held across all age groups. We found that individuals perceive that there is still a process of discrimination against people like them. They still think in class terms (Figure 3 over).

Yet this sense of difference does not translate to affiliations with collective or class-defined organisations or institutions, a finding that we explore in more detail below.

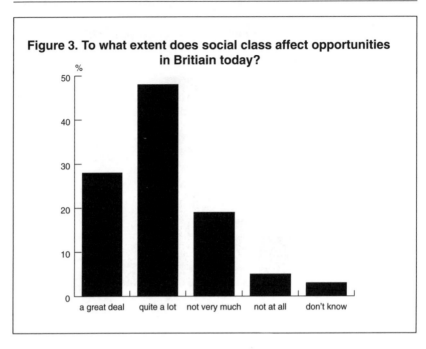

Figure 3. To what extent does social class affect opportunities in Britiain today?

This suggests strongly that political parties should not believe their own rhetoric about living in a classless society. Basildonians believe they are class-bound, but do not wish to be patronised about it, and would not identify with class-based interests in deciding which way to vote. Tony Blair has recently made upward social mobility a central goal for his government. Our analysis suggests that the general goal may find widespread sympathy, but that it will be difficult (as it has proved) for politicians to find a positive language which captures and mobilises the sense of unfairness or unfulfilled aspiration which many feel.

Class without struggle
When we probed what class meant to people, they suggested that it was a historical and cultural identity, rather than a political one. Many respondents talked reverentially of their links with the old East End. The world that Basildonians sought to escape, they have recreated symbolically as an idyllic working-class community – or at least a byword for neighbourliness.

The historian EP Thompson famously characterised the beginning of the nineteenth century as a period in which there was class struggle without class. At the beginning of the twenty-first, we could invert that proposition and say that there is class without class struggle. While the perspective of class shapes a cultural outlook, it does not define social and political views.

This detachment was similarly reflected in how people viewed trade unions. Most of those who identified themselves as working class did not belong to a union.

In 1997 32 per cent of respondents were TU members, the same figure as for the country as a whole in 1995.[12] This proportion is still quite high by European standards, although the same publication points out that the UK has suffered the greatest haemorrhaging of union membership out of the thirteen European nations studied, losing 30 per cent of union members over the period from 1955–95.

Unionisation is lower among the young (Figure 4). The 1992 survey showed union membership increasing with age from 27 per cent in the 25 to 34 group to 40 per cent of the 55+ age group. Trade union member-

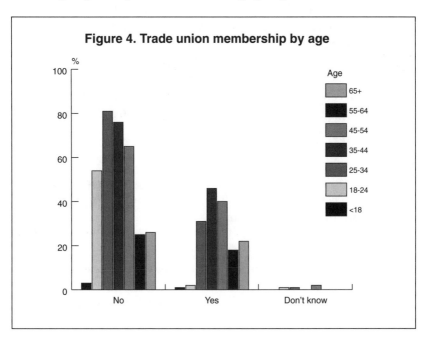

Figure 4. Trade union membership by age

ship was more characteristic of older workers and the retired. The 1997 survey figures, given below, showed even more dramatic decreases, with young skilled workers being fifteen times less likely to be in a union than the over-35 age group.

The most significant finding in this area, however, was not that union membership was low, but that people saw no relationship between unions and class. Rather, they viewed them pragmatically, without any strong feeling for or against.

Indeed, among non-members, only 5 per cent cited an in-principle objection to TU membership. On the other hand there was no pent-up urge to join unions. Only one person felt that joining a union would damage their job prospects.

These findings suggest that the recent slight rise in UK union membership is a pragmatic shift rather than an increasing sense of collective consciousness. It was not ever thus: one of our respondents remarked on the close connection between working-class communities and trade unions in the 1960s:

> 'In Dagenham unions were much more militant. In Basildon expectations were different. Attendance was never great, but people went religiously.'

Today's trade-union meetings mostly struggle to reach a quorum. Individuals' concerns these days are likely to be dealt with in a one-to-one meeting with an official, not resolved through public debate and a vote.

Work

Is work becoming more important to identity and aspiration? Not really: only 9 per cent of our 1997 respondents put job or career as the most important thing in their lives.

However, we found young people entirely at ease with the new flexible labour market, expecting to change jobs at least two to four times: there was no assumption of a 'job for life'. They were more likely to travel to work and happier to work and live outside of Basildon, even outside Britain. They were confident and aspirant about their ability to get on at work. When asked what they would find most satisfying, being good at their job was their first choice.

Basildonians live close to their place of work. Seventy per cent of the employed respondents worked in Basildon itself and a quarter of the remainder travelled less than ten miles to work. But they do not find community through work.

We asked how often people socialised with their workmates (366 respondents were employed and the figures given in the next few paragraphs are valid percentages of this total). Just over a fifth (22 per cent) socialised more than once a week; a further 16 per cent did so once a week. Most people met up with work colleagues socially far less often: for a fifth (22 per cent) it was once a month, and a third (33 per cent) met their workmates socially even less frequently (Figure 5).

When we looked at what kinds of social activities were involved, it became clear that work-based collective social engagement is highly attenuated.

By far the most popular activity (35 per cent) with workmates was a visit to the pub. Going for a drink exemplified the casual nature of work-

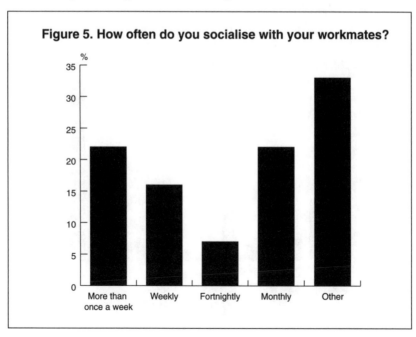

Figure 5. How often do you socialise with your workmates?

based socialising, in which people would meet for a few hours before going their separate ways. There was no sense of shared interest or activity above and beyond the immediate and transient moments of conviviality.

Other social activities

If Basildonians are not bothered about socialising with their workmates, neither are they attached to other kinds of leisure community (Figure 6).

Aside from the pub, the other frequent leisure activities of Basildonians take them swimming, clubbing and to the gym, where they share space with fellow users in an accident of timing rather than by any specific arrangement. Also popular are the even less sociable pastimes of cycling, walking, gardening and reading.

The point is not that any of these activities is bad, but that the balance of social activity in Basildon is skewed fundamentally towards individualised activities – to the practical exclusion of communal and even joint interests.

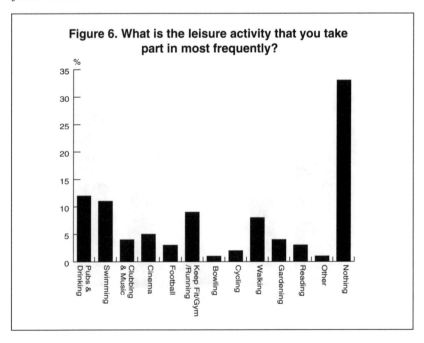

Figure 6. What is the leisure activity that you take part in most frequently?

We found further confirmation of this trend when we looked at club membership in Basildon. More than half of 1997 respondents (55 per cent) said they did not belong to any club. No one bothered to mention their trade union membership in this context and only one or two mentioned their church. For many others who were members of leisure centres, their membership gave access to facilities and resources but told us nothing about any shared set of experiences.

It seems that neither work nor leisure gives a social focus to life in Basildon. Even football failed to hit the spot, despite the numbers of people sporting West Ham shirts. We did include 'your football team' as a possible answer to 'What is the most important thing in your life?' Two respondents gave it as their second choice; a further thirteen put it third! So what gives meaning and cohesion to the lives of people in Basildon? The answer, overwhelmingly, is: the family.

Family

Throughout our 1997 survey we found confirmation and reconfirmation of the centrality of the family to the lives of Basildon's C2s. This

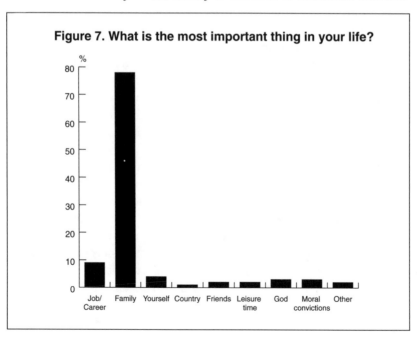

Figure 7. What is the most important thing in your life?

represented a significant shift from the traditional model in which skilled workers tended to orient their social lives around their workplace and work colleagues.

We asked what was the most important thing in people's lives and the response was clear and consistent.

More than three-quarters (78 per cent) selected family as the most important thing in their lives (Figure 7). The respondents were given a list of options from which they were asked to select three in order of importance for them. Only 8 per cent did not place family among their top three choices. No other single facet of our interviewees' lives even reached 10 per cent in terms of its primary importance.

Recent analysis and debate has canvassed the notion that friendship may have replaced the family as the crucial form and substance of mutual support and social solidarity. Our evidence suggests otherwise: family is the cornerstone of social life for Basildonians.

The key message in this finding is that Basildonians seem to be repositioning the balance of their lives between public and private concerns. As their affinity with other forms of identity or solidarity (class, work, trade union) fades, they have placed even greater emphasis on their family lives.

This is not to say that the form and nature of family relations are fixed or frozen. Far from it. When interviewees referred to the family as the bedrock of social interaction, it was not exclusively or even primarily the nuclear family they meant. Divorce, remarriage, single-parent families, step-parents, widows and widowers were all there: the plethora of forms that family relations now take is integral to people's understanding of family.

Elsewhere this phenomenon has been termed the 'negotiated' or 'networked' family.[13] Our findings chime with these and various other recent discussions which describe a new interface between individuals in domestic circumstances and wider sets of social relationships

The Basildonians in our survey expressed themselves through the medium of family relationships. The family was the source and dynamic of their hopes, aspirations, security and comfort. This was expressed by respondents across the generations, who would talk about what they wanted for their families. Its apogee is Alf Dove's vision of Basildon being a place where families could get their own house. It is there in the interview with Tracey Clark (see page 32), who wants a large family but is haunted by the possibility of being a single mum.

According to Basildon Trends (1997), the town has a higher proportion of single parents (4.4 per cent) than Essex (2.9 per cent), or the UK average (3.7 per cent). Single-parent families more than doubled in the eighties, rising from 1,332 in 1981 to 2, 750 in 1991.[14] But both as individuals and as family members Basildonians have an uncomfortable sense that the security that is defined through the family is threatened. It is threatened because the circumstances that enable the family to exercise its role, cannot be kept in place merely individual effort. They are painfully aware that the preconditions for security are beyond their control. Neither do they have any confidence that anyone else is in control: they can identify no institution or set of values that can insert stability and certainty into their lives, to allay their fears or resolve their insecurities and tensions.

We saw this concern about the uncontrollability of life again when we asked more generally about people's quality of life and prospects.

Personally optimistic

Residents of Basildon were more personally optimistic about their own situation but more pessimistic about the trajectory of the society in which they live. They regard improvements in the quality of their lives as the result of their own efforts and not the consequences of government action. The number of Basildonians who considered that their own lives had improved over the previous five years was 47 per cent (Figure 8). In 1992 the figure was 46 per cent. In statistical terms this is not a significant change. In 1997 only 21 per cent of respondents believed their quality of life had deteriorated over the previous five years. This is a drop from the 26 per cent who believed this to be the case in 1992. 1992 was the fag end of Thatcherism and a time of economic uncertainty for Basildon. The 1997 election came after a period of recovery for the area. The changed economic outlook makes surprisingly little difference. Basildonians retained their personal optimism in 1992 and the economic upturn from 1992 to 1997 does not seem to have made much difference to it, perhaps because it has not had a positive impact on real wages. Yet while Basildon turned an economic corner and unemployment levels fell, almost two fifths of

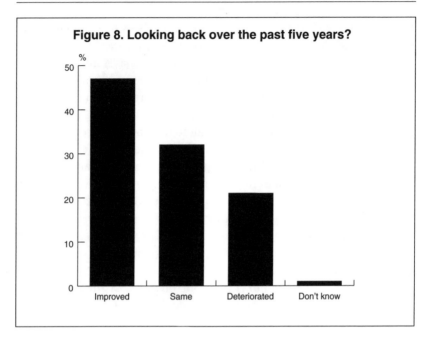

Figure 8. Looking back over the past five years?

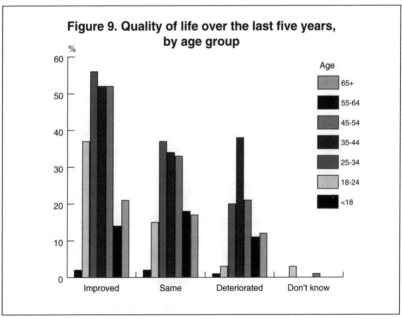

Figure 9. Quality of life over the last five years, by age group

respondents (39 per cent) could not find a good thing to say about the Conservative government that had been in office throughout the five year period, a marked increase from the 24 per cent who held the same opinion in 1992.

There are variations within this generally positive outlook. Nine out of ten of the 18-24 age group felt their conditions had stayed the same or improved. Among middle-aged groups the proportion dropped to 70 per cent (Figure 9).

The positive tone we found among Basildonians extended to optimism about their prospects (Figure 10).

A third of respondents in both years (34 per cent in 1992 and 32 per cent in 1997) felt that things would stay the same, while the number who felt things would get worse dropped dramatically from 18 per cent to 7 per cent. Again, the age breakdown shows the optimism of youth declining in late middle age.

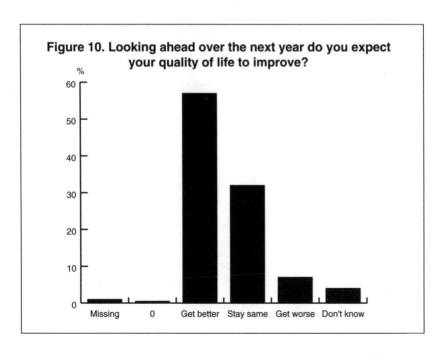

Figure 10. Looking ahead over the next year do you expect your quality of life to improve?

Portrait 2: Tracey Clark: Basildon Girl

Tracey Clark exemplifies the Basildon of today as much as Alf Dove represents the Basildon of the 1950s and 1960s.

'I've lived here thirteen years, it's an all-right place. I've got an older sister. She's in marketing. She has been to university and has a degree. She is 23, I'm 21. My dad was in engineering and my mum was a nurse. I'm doing an apprenticeship in electronic engineering. I get to study for an HNC as well as do placements and work experience and I get an apprenticeship at the end. I get experience and education at the same time.'

She is ambitious and independent but is sceptical about the influence of Basildon, the council or the schools:

'I've done things for myself. My life is better because I've improved it by working hard, saving money, getting a car, doing stuff myself – that's my way of improvement.

'My school let me down. They didn't help me at all. I got by on my own . Now there are a lot of private schools about. Everyone is going to them. If you've got the money you get the education. I got all my GCSEs but that was through all my own hard work...

'I can't see the council doing anything. It's like the Bell Tower – it's there but irrelevant. The big change is the Festival Leisure Park restaurants, pubs and a bowling alley. If you live in Basildon and you haven't got a car you can't really get anywhere, so a big complex like that does attract people. Suddenly Basildon's on the map. Before there wasn't really much to come here for. The shopping centre has always been there for me. There's Lakeside – you can go out to that but that's not different to what you've got back here.'

She hasn't heard of any Tory policies: *'I don't really remember any. I never took much notice at all.'*

She supports no political party: *'When it comes round to voting, me and those that I go with don't take much interest in it. In the last election I voted for Labour. I've never been Conservative.'*

She replies with horror to the suggestion that she should ever join a political party or be active: *'Oh No!'*

She isn't a trade union member. Though she sees herself as working class this is a tag she wants to leave behind:

'No one offered me any information about a trade union. I never really thought about it.' Would she join, if asked? *'It depends what it's all about, what benefits there are, how it would help me.*

'I'm working class. If you come from a background where your parents don't encourage you, you're going to get stuck in your class. But if you try to work yourself up, push yourself.... I suppose you always get put in a category but you can always work your way out of it.'

Tracey sees coming from Basildon new town as an embarrassment:

'I wouldn't say I'm from Basildon. I'd probably just say Essex. It's because of what they think about the name. It was always supposed to be the new town. If I met someone on holiday they'd just stereotype you. I'd say, I'm from London but not Essex – they'd immediately get a smile on their face...Some people do live up to it. If I had a choice of where to move, I wouldn't come to Basildon...'

She values her family, friends and getting on in her career:

'The traditional family is disappearing. I've got a traditional family so that's important to me. I've always had people around me, always there to lean on. But I've got friends who've just got one parent and they're quite happy enough. I hope I'm not [a single mum]... I really do hope I'm not. Single parents can be just as good .... they can bring their child up as good as anyone else.

'I'd like to be good at my job. To advance my career. If you don't have ambition you can't do anything. Education usually backs you up a lot. I want to get on. My sister's the same as me, she's ambitious.'

On crime and drugs she is pragmatic:

'It all comes down to survival; getting through stuff. Drugs are just there. They've just grown up with them. These days it's just a way of life.'

Thoughts about herself and the future:

'Work is only about a 15-minute ride. I think I'll stay there a couple of years. It's a really good job. I don't have to get a train to go to London; then again, if that's where the money is...

'I hope to have a family but also keep working. I just like the idea of a big family... but I'll probably change my mind after the first one.

'It's weird, the way work is changing. Jobs are getting harder, education's getting harder. Young people have got advantages, like growing up with computers. They've got disadvantages in other ways - in getting a job. They are going to find it really hard. They're going to be pushed so much to get an education.

'It's the best here because there's more opportunities; now you've got an industrial site there's more jobs.'

Broadly pessimistic

But personal optimism did not translate beyond the bounds of local life. When interviewees were asked to think about opportunities for the next generation, a much more equivocal perspective emerged. 46 per cent thought the next generation would have fewer opportunities compared to 40 per cent who thought they would have more (Figure 11). The sense of foreboding became more pronounced in response to a question about whether Britain was becoming a worse or a better place to live (Figure 12).

One in twenty thought it was getting much better, while three times as many (15 per cent) thought it was getting much worse. Just under a third thought the country was getting a little better, but they were matched by another third believing it was getting a little worse; the remaining fifth saw no discernible change.

The imbalance in outlook here is striking: people feel their own lives are improving while simultaneously believing that the possibilities for the next generation are less rosy and society in general is getting worse. It would be hard to find a more poignant expression of the dislo-

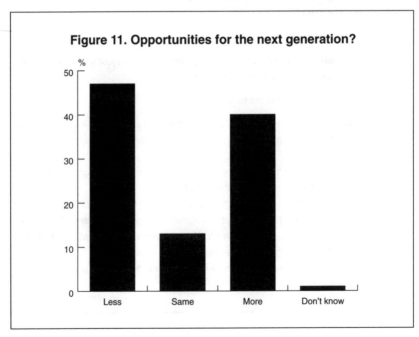

Figure 11. Opportunities for the next generation?

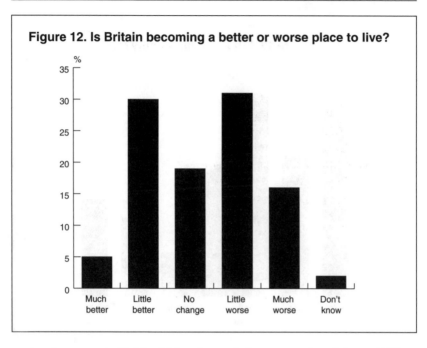

Figure 12. Is Britain becoming a better or worse place to live?

cation between individual identity and the sense of social possibility.

This contrast is perhaps best explained in terms of a general contemporary phenomenon: the inability to connect an individual project or set of hopes and aspirations with collective fortunes and endeavours. This disconnection helps to explain why people have refocused on personal and family relations, and why the emphasis on the local, at the expense of the wider world or more abstract communities, also seems to have grown.

The local : their hearts belong to Basildon

Our survey revealed a strong sense of local identity, of being from Basildon. More than a fifth (22 per cent) thought of themselves as belonging to the town. This is almost as many as those who identified with England and many more than those who chose Europe. The same proportion would stay in Basildon rather than live anywhere else (Figure 13, over).

This sense of local belonging seems to come before more abstract issues of national identity. Our survey showed that the prospect of a

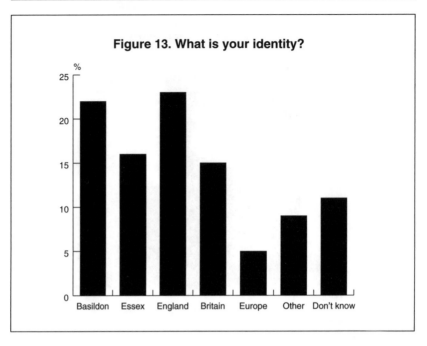

Figure 13. What is your identity?

newly militant English nationalism emerging, partly in response to the perceived threat of Europe, seems unlikely. Respondents confirmed little interest in adopting a European identity (but also little active hostility to it). More importantly Basildonians were telling us something else: that the polarity of current debate is wrong because it completely omits the level of identity which is most precious to them: locality.

Does Basildon's wider sense of pessimism matter? It does, because the absence of a common sense of purpose eventually undermines the belief in individual potential. The old identities no longer bring people together. Individuals are thrown back on their own devices, investing all their hopes in their personal endeavour supported by the security of their family relationships. A lack of confidence in broader public life has a negative effect, in the long run, on individual wellbeing.

Against objective measures such as income, Basildonians are not doing that well. Their approach to achieving quality of life – achieving a degree of economic security or gaining access to more positional goods, is based on acting alone, rather than engaging with others in similar circumstances to forge collective strategies for change. Success means being the 'best survivor', with only the family to rely on.

This presents an acute problem for policy-makers, because it reduces the range of tools and resources which can be used in trying to improve people's circumstances. Government intervention is likely to be received, not as provision of more opportunity and security, but as imposition on individual lifestyles and identities.

The quality of public life is not sustained merely by resource provision but through participation and active adherence to a public agenda. In Basildon this seems to be largely absent.

4. Explaining Labour's victory

Basildon first came to prominence among psephologists almost by accident. In the Fifties, the constituency of Billericay – which at the time included Basildon – set records for being the fastest to return its general election results. Over the years, as Appendix 1 shows, Basildon proved to be an accurate barometer of national voting trends. During the long reign of Thatcherism, the constituency took on, through the media prism, the personality of its outspoken Thatcherite MP David Amess, and when Amess was returned safely in 1992 in one of the earliest declarations, excited political commentators heralded it as confirmation of Labour's imminent defeat. If Labour could not take Basildon, the argument went, it was possible that Thatcherism had wrought some deeper, more permanent change in the attitudes and outlooks of working-class people.

From what we have learnt about Basildonians, that argument is false.

Thatcherism was skin deep. There was no rooted ideological shift in the outlook of Basildonians. For a short period, the rhetoric of Thatcherism seemed to offer the material improvements that matched local people's aspirations. But their commitment and enthusiasm vanished with the more difficult times at the end of the Eighties. Basildon's people today hold no more rooted loyalties to New Labour.

In 1992 and 1997 we sought people's views on the importance of various issues, and whether the government had done a good job. We found that 'popular conservatism' had had little impact. The clearest illustration was the lack of endorsement for policies such as privatisation and share ownership, even in 1992. The political shifts in the 1980s

Figure 14. Support in Basildon for government policies, 1992 and 1997

Government Policy	Support (%) 1992	Support (%) 1997	Difference % points
Home ownership	40	36	-4
Privatisation	9	9	0
Cut income taxes	32	15	-17
Curbed TU power	18	13	-5
Share ownership	4	8	+4
Restricted immigration	31	11	-20
Allowing schools to opt out	16	14	-2
Strengthened law and order	17	10	-7
None of these	24	39	+15

had much more to do with a rejection of Labour than a positive embrace of Thatcherism.

By 1997 local distaste for government policies had hardened. Thirty-nine per cent of respondents felt unable to nominate a single policy among those listed, as being the best thing the government had done (Figure 14). The equivalent figure in 1992 had been 24 per cent.

The most popular policy was home ownership: 36 per cent of the 1997 sample said it was the best thing the Conservatives had done in the last 18 years. This is the only flagship policy of the 1980s which has left an imprint on the lives of the people of Basildon. It was a policy that gave practical expression to the sense of independence and security they seek.

One of the most significant changes during the 1990s appeared to be a shift in attitudes to race. Support for restricting immigration dropped by 20 per cent. The fear we had found in 1992 of being overtaken or pushed out by other races had begun to disappear. This finding was supported by answers to other questions. It could reflect the reality that there was little immigration to Britain in the late 1990s. Or it could be that racism in the old sense is no longer an issue, surfacing mainly among older generations as part of the folk memories of working-class London in the 1950s and 1960s.

Support (with and without reservations) for anti-racist laws was fairly static, increasing from 86 per cent to 89 per cent. But this masks

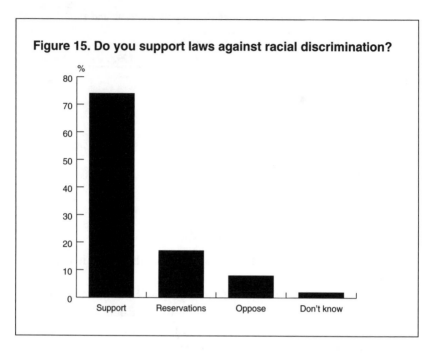

Figure 15. Do you support laws against racial discrimination?

a massive change: in 1992, 36 per cent 'fully supported' laws against racial discrimination; in 1997 the proportion had doubled to 73 per cent (Figure 15).

Similarly, opposition to anti-racist laws had halved, dropping from 19 to 9 per cent.

There was still a predominant feeling in 1997 that Britain gave too much support to immigrants (51 per cent). But this figure had dropped from 64 per cent in 1992. Those believing that Britain gave the right amount of help went up from 19 to 28 per cent. But the numbers who felt Britain did not give enough support almost doubled (13 per cent compared with 7 per cent in 1992).

These figures provide clear evidence of how the politics of race changed during the 1990s. This is not to say that racial discrimination was eradicated, more that hostility to the Asian and Afro-Caribbean communities ceased to be a credible political rallying point. The residual individual prejudice expressed in certain Basildon pubs is a far cry from the explicit racism we met on the streets in 1992.

Interview with policy-makers 1

'What I wanted to say as a follow-up to the meeting in town is on the question of racism, when you picked up that we were and are no longer a racist society in Basildon. I take issue with that. It may not be there in the research that you carried out but I would say this. If you go to the Basildon clubs then you will hear the racism going on. And you'll see some of the people subjected to it. It may not be as blatant and open as you might hear elsewhere ... my perception of it was in terms of not actually being directed against people from ethnic minorities but a willingness to tell racist jokes , engage in racist banter and feel obliged to be 'in', because if you're not, you're 'out' and supporting something that we don't. .....I have no evidence to back that up other than the evenings I have spent in Basildon's pubs and clubs.'

Q. Are you more sensitive to it now? Is it objectively worse or are more people more sensitive to it?

'No, I don't think I'm more sensitive to it now than five or ten years ago. I think there is probably a general increase in awareness and particularly in core councils because of the Stephen Lawrence inquiry and everything else.'

Q. I think what it means is it doesn't become a political issue; people don't decide to vote on the basis of race.

'No, I don't think it affects their lives in any way, shape or form other than the fact that it's something to have a laugh and joke about. I don't think they make decisions based upon it at all. It's just quite prevalent, you know, if you listen to any comedian telling jokes in any pub, whereas on the TV or elsewhere racism has disappeared. Round here it hasn't.'

Our survey was undertaken before the recent furore over asylum-seekers. While we believe the responses support the view that the powerful impact made by the 'race card' in the 1970s and 1980s will not re-emerge in the same form, we could not rule out the possibility of an outbreak of renewed fear and hostility arising from the aggressive rhetoric now being used by some politicians.

Another Thatcherite flagship policy – income tax cuts – also seems to have lost the support of Basildonians, down from 32 to 15 per cent backing. An apparent reduction in support for stronger law enforcement is more ambiguous: this could reflect a feeling either that too much or too little was being done. We certainly discovered an increased fear of crime (see page 51).

The Thatcherite project to curb the power of trade unions received little support by 1997, largely because the trade unions had ceased to be relevant to most people's lives.

So if by 1997 Basildon had stopped caring about the Thatcherite agenda, what did it now care about? We asked what was of most concern to people's families? The answer came back: education, up from 28 per cent of respondents in 1992 to 45 per cent in 1997. Unemployment remained high on the list, still commanding 53 per cent of concern. In general, Basildonians' concerns begin to mirror more closely a social-democratic agenda rather than a radical minimalist-state one. But this does not give the green light to a return to the old politics of left and right. Even priority issues such as health and education are being viewed within a new political landscape which presents a challenge to all policy-makers.

Thatcherism has left no legacy in the shape of prominent individuals or new institutions that could carry forward its key tenets. But one achievement did endure: it dealt a death-blow to important forms of collectivism in society. Thatcherism enjoyed negative success as the corrosive agent which broke down the vestigial certainties of old forms of social life. What has emerged in the late 1990s is a landscape in which individuals stand out in isolated relief, without much reference to each other and with only minimal relationships to other institutions and organisations.

5. Real priorities

We asked people to tell us which three issues were of most concern to them and their families (Figure 16). In 1997 they singled out health (60 per cent), unemployment (53 per cent) and education (45 per cent).

Issues such as immigration, Aids and inflation were of little concern to the respondents. A key Thatcherite policy – the poll tax – had aroused hostility in 1992 but was now low down the list of worries. The two other issues that did attract concern were mortgage repayments and the environment. About a fifth (18 per cent) of respondents included mortgage repayments in their choices. Fifty-seven per cent of our respondents were home owners. This figure is out of alignment with Basildon District (which includes Billericay and Wickford), but almost

Figure 16. What issue is of most concern to you and your family?		
Per cent citing the following themes:		
Issue	1992	1997
Unemployment	59	53
Environment	26	34
Inflation	14	14
Poll Tax	30	7
Crime	36	47
Education	27	45
Mortgage Repayments	17	17
Immigration	7	3
Health	45	60
Aids	10	2
Other	2	2

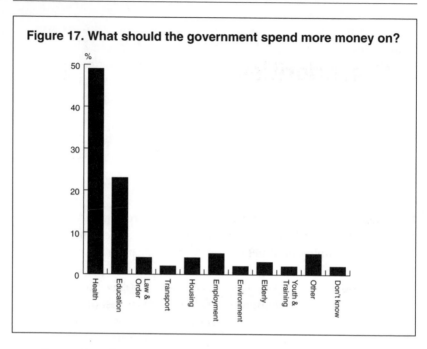

Figure 17. What should the government spend more money on?

exactly matches the home ownership figure for the New Town. The fear of losing the security of home ownership, an aspiration of earlier Basildonians, was real enough.

About a third (35 per cent) voiced concern about the environment. From other of the survey questions we conclude that the worry here was about the immediate, local built environment rather than a more general articulation of "green" views. Basildonians were thinking about transport, roads, green spaces, litter and the town centre (see page 46).

We asked the respondents to select one priority for higher government spending. We offered no prompts to them. The results confirmed and accentuated their expressed concerns and priorities. Sixty per cent had nominated health as one of their top three concerns and 49 pere cent made it a choice for more spending (Figure 17). Forty-five per cent had made education one of their top three concerns and for 22 per cent it was their number one priority for more spending. It seems that health attracts the most concern and perhaps a hope that greater funding will produce results.

Although more people put unemployment (53 per cent) as a concern than education (45 per cent) this is not reflected in priorities for more spending. A number of factors may account for this. Education is itself seen as a self-improving way of enhancing employment prospects. Unemployment has declined mainly because of an influx of service sector jobs. Perhaps the high concern with unemployment owes more to residual fears for security while the lower prioritisation on spending for employment reflects a lack of credibility for government job creation programmes (see chapter six).

The gap was even greater between the concern about crime and a desire for more spending on law and order. Forty-seven per cent of respondents listed crime as one of their top three concerns, but only 4 per cent selected it as the priority area for increased government spending.

We should reiterate here that our respondents were not prompted in their replies to what the government should spend less on. We took all the responses and grouped them accordingly. This includes the specific use of the term 'fat cats'. A number of respondents did not give a reply,

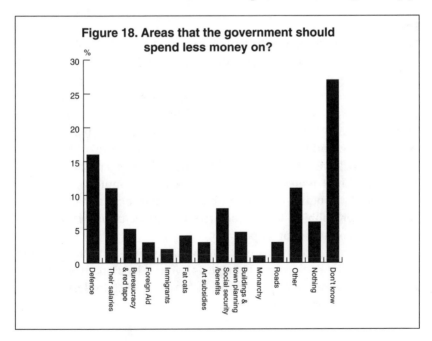

Figure 18. Areas that the government should spend less money on?

Just under 26 per cent of our sample, for those who did, there was a discernible theme: antagonism to the institutions of government. The aggregate desire to cut spending on 'their salaries', 'bureaucracy and red tape' and ' fat cats' constituted nearly a fifth of the respondents (19 per cent) – or a third of those who voiced an opinion of any sort (Figure 18). A further 3 per cent wanted to cut art subsidies. This may seem a strange pre-occupation. We think of it as a hangover form an earlier dispute over the Towngate Theatre, regarded by many Basildonians in 1992, as a white elephant. This old story was then given a new lease of life by controversy over the National Lottery funding for the Royal Opera.

This may provide further ballast for the unpalatable message: Basildonians feel disengaged from and mistrustful of political and administrative institutions. If they think about them at all, they believe they are a waste of money. If things are going well they put it down to their own efforts. Basildonians are eager for the extension of provision, notably in health and education, but suspicious or cynical of the will-ingness of political institutions to come up with the goods. The political class are suspected of providing only for themselves.

Local priorities

We started off by asking 'What do you least like about Basildon at present?' The responses were all unprompted. The single biggest response (13 per cent) was 'crime and violence' (Figure 19). But crime was not the main concern. Far more people were anxious about their immediate built environment. A major rebuilding programme, in and around the main civic and shopping centre, was going on at the time of our survey, and has undoubtedly fuelled specific local concerns Yet we do not believe it fully accounts for the weight of anxiety directed at the bundle of issues to do with the local environment. Taking an aggregate of the building work, the built-up environment, bad housing, squalor, litter, rubbish, lack of facilities and traffic/transport, the level of concern comes out at 42 per cent.

We believe this confirms our interpretation of the concern noted above with "the environment" (page 44), voiced by 35 per cent. This is no desire for lower petrol emissions, but rather a wish for less rubbish, more green spaces and more roads.

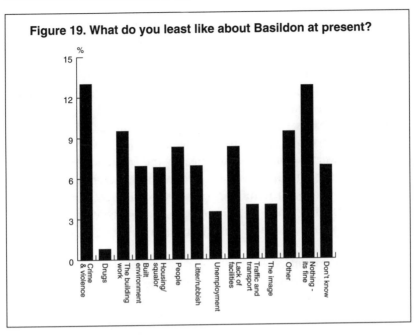

Figure 19. What do you least like about Basildon at present?

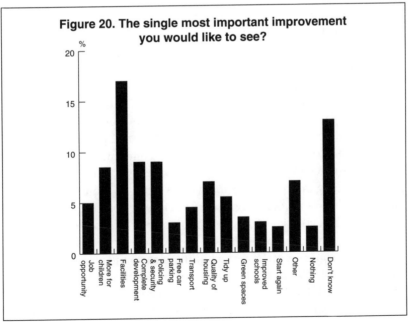

Figure 20. The single most important improvement you would like to see?

We found similar worries when we asked people to nominate the single most important improvement they would like to see in the town (Figure 20).

These responses were also unprompted. Nine per cent wanted the building developments to be completed. There was a desire to see better facilities, free car parking, transport, improved housing, a tidy up and green spaces. Far fewer people (3 per cent) identified schools and hospitals as the most important improvement. We think this was low, given the powerful concerns about health and education that we have already noted. It is telling us that Basildonians' concerns about health and education, are not reducible to the bricks and mortar of schools and hospitals. They worry in a more general way about lack of future opportunities, and about their life chances in a climate of uncertainty.

Fear of unemployment

Fear of unemployment is the most clearly articulated anxiety about the future, as well as the hardest phenomenon to interpret.

It featured emphatically in our 1992 survey, cited as a concern by 59 per cent. Five years later the fear remained high at 53 per cent. But the fear is substantially out of alignment with local realities.

In 1992 Basildon's unemployment rate was, at 10 per cent, higher than the national average. It peaked at 12 per cent in 1993, and had declined to 4 per cent by 1998. At the time of our second survey it stood at 6 per cent. All of our 1997 respondents were employed.

How can we explain this fear? There is some indication that young people are particularly susceptible to it. Their worries about unemployment ran higher than the average in 1997, at 62 per cent. (Only the 45-plus age group matched this level of concern.) And others are certainly worried on their behalf. When we asked: 'What is the biggest problem facing young people today?', 53 per cent nominated unemployment (Figure 21). Nothing else came close, despite the town having lived with the extensive publicity surrounding the death of Leah Betts from Ecstasy in November 1995.

These was some suggestion – including from young people themselves – that their attitudes might be a problem, a possible contributory factor to their perceived lack of employability. Eleven per cent of respondents mentioned 'their attitudes' as the biggest problem for young people.

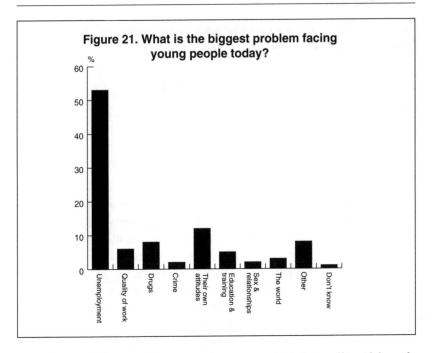

Figure 21. What is the biggest problem facing young people today?

But none of these makes sense when set against the reality. Although there are pockets of concern, Basildon does not have a serious youth unemployment problem. Long-term youth unemployment is virtually non-existent. Eighteen months after our survey, only 61 young people fell into this category.

It could be that a general sense of insecurity translates in employment terms to fears of short-term or part-time contracts interspersed with period of unemployment and job seeking. Yet we discovered elsewhere in our survey work that Basildonians welcomed the new flexible workplace and frequent job changes. The prospect of the changed workplace was accepted, not feared.

So we are left to conclude that people's widespread fear is a residual concern from earlier times, a menacing shadow haunting people whose attachment to their town is founded upon the promise of opportunity and self-improvement.

Figure 22. Is there any political party that genuinely represents your interests and concerns?

A comparison of the 1992 and 1997 Survey Findings

	1992 %	1997 %
YES	44	36
NO	50	57
Don't Know	5	6

After politics

In 1992 37 per cent of respondents told us they were very or quite satisfied with the British political system. Forty-eight per cent were not. In 1997 satisfaction levels had risen to 52 per cent and dissatisfaction had dropped to 41 per cent. Is this good news for political parties in general and New Labour in particular? We don't think so.

Set alongside the magnitude of New Labour's victory in 1997 and the sense of possibility that it supposedly released, these shifts in satisfaction levels seem almost inconsequential.

And even at the height of Labour's post election popularity we were discerning signs that political parties were failing to capture the hearts and minds of Basildon's voters. As Figure 22 shows, there has been a clear decline in party support, notwithstanding the huge general election vote for New Labour.

Almost six out of ten (57 per cent) said that no political party genuinely represented their interests and concerns (Figure 23). Out of those who did nominate a party, more than half of them plumped for Labour. Not surprisingly the Conservative Party did very badly: the 13 per cent who felt represented by the Tories was a lower figure than for the LibDems (18 per cent of the sub-sample).

There is no good news here for politicians of any hue. We found that those who had abandoned their previous allegiances in favour of no party were drawn almost equally from the ranks of Labour (5 per cent) and Conservative (4 per cent) supporters. Labour's disenchanted stressed their former affinity with Old Labour.

Far from there being evidence of any allegiance to New Labour, we found that a seepage of political identification among traditional Labour supporters was not being replaced by the active support of those

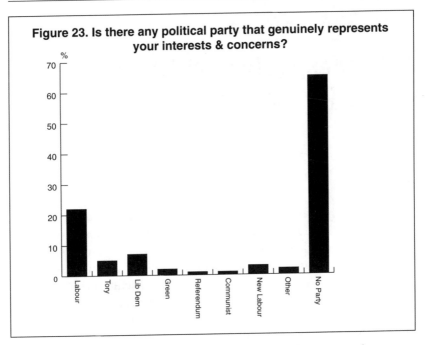

Figure 23. Is there any political party that genuinely represents your interests & concerns?

whose votes put Tony Blair into Downing Street. These voters have very little faith in anything other than themselves.

Basildonians put health and education at the top of their national agenda. They prioritise the environment and amenities locally. Crime appears to straddle the local-national divide, but as the council has identified in its own studies, concerns are closely related to people's experience of their immediate environment. The commonest single crime worry is joyriding, and the biggest social irritant is parking in the wrong place.

In among this continued preoccupation with social issues there is a pervasive sense that the present framework of political institutions, especially at national level, cannot deal effectively with them.

There may be a reflection here of the further sense, noted in numerous recent studies, that the existing institutions cannot be effective and are therefore illegitimate.[15] These institutions suffer from both declining membership, in the case of parties, and lower participation in the case of trade unions and civic organisations. At the same time there are no alternatives waiting in the wings.

6. Challenges for politicians and policy-makers

The first thing politicians and policy-makers must appreciate is the extent to which people have allowed themselves to become detached from formal political institutions and wider civic arrangements. Against this backdrop politicians will need a different set of reponses to address people's shifting sense of identity and their particular priorities.

At present one institution stands as a bulwark against social isolation: the family. People's identities are most powerfully expressed through the family, and a potential pride in the local.

Policy-makers need to recognise that the continuity of concern for matters such as education and health is not simply or primarily about resources but bound up with Basildonians' belief in the importance of having some control over their own lives, in order to be able to get on.

In this chapter we look in more detail at what education means to Basildonians and how policy initiatives relate to these concerns. We then look at how local policy-makers are trying to re-engage with the citizen through the theory and practice of joined-up thinking.

Getting the education message right

We found that during the 1990s education rose in importance to the people of Basildon. This finding emerged strongly from our surveys in two ways:. It was, alongside health, the most prioritised area for increased government spending; and it was the factor people identified as most important in promoting their personal and career development. This latter and more individualised desire for education is clearly linked to work but is not always purely vocational. There was some emphasis on the value of something like a more traditional liberal education.

We found the desire for education vague in that it was not linked to any particular policy demands in the way that the first generation of Basildonians argued for comprehensive schools. Nor did people suggest any particular remedial measures to improve the state of their schools. Where criticisms were made, the target was often teachers – and again, the comments tended to be vague. Teachers were held to have 'let people down' or to 'be against change'. No one in our sample mentioned a particular course or training that they wanted to undertake. The closest we could get was a 'degree' or a 'college course'.

Is increased spending the issue?

When we asked 1992 respondents to identify their three top priorities, 27 per cent mentioned education. In 1997 the proportion was 45 per cent. Overall in 1997 education came fourth behind health (top with 60 per cent), unemployment and crime. But it had the largest increase, at 18 percentage points, in the level of concern, matched only by an increase of 15 percentage points in worries about health.

The high level of popular concern with education did not translate directly into demands for more government funding. People singled out health and education as their top spending targets, but not straightforwardly. The 60 per cent concern for health turned into a 49 per cent desire for more spending. And the 45 per cent concern for education produced a 22 per cent wish for increased government cash. Could these gaps of 11 percentage points and 23 percentage points respectively, reflect an attitude which held that you could improve the health service by giving it more money, but not necessarily education? Our qualitative interviews and discussions confirmed that this was the case (see below).

Is training the issue?

There was little evidence that the concern with education was related to young people's training needs. Only 2 per cent of our respondents felt that the government should spend more on youth training. Only 5 per cent identified education and training as a problem for young people. Some thought that this sort of training came with a job. There was no concern that a lack of basic job training would bring about unemployment. People's worries were, rather, connected to the experience of the changes in the contemporary workplace and the decline of the traditional way of bettering your pay and conditions through trade union activity.

When we asked 'What do you think is the best way of advancing your career?' 52 per cent said education and training (Figure 24). This contrasts with 31 per cent in our national survey of attitudes to work.[16] If we add 'Staff Development' to this we get 56 per cent compared with 37 per cent in the finding of an earlier, national study.[17] For a further 15 per cent of Basildonians, career advancement was seen as coming with a change of job, which shows some self-confidence among our respondents in their individual abilities to get on. But so does their faith in education and training. In fact, such highly individualised attitudes are a new phenomenon.

In the 1950s and 1960s education was hardly mentioned in studies of the skilled worker. In the 1968 classic study of embourgeoisement, *The Affluent Worker: Industrial attitudes and behaviour*,[18] education and

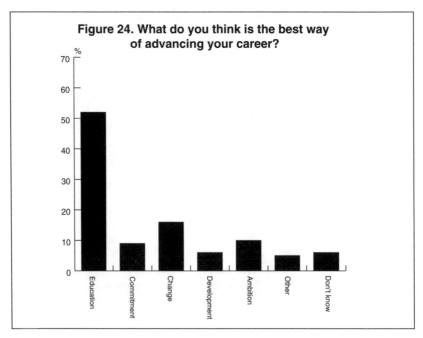

Figure 24. What do you think is the best way of advancing your career?

training arise solely in the specific context of the possibility of becoming a foreman. In Goldthorpe et al's sample of semi-skilled and skilled workers, 85 per cent left school at fourteen or younger and 15 per cent had any subsequent part-time vocational training. This is a distinct contrast with our group of skilled workers in Basildon, all of whom had undertaken training.

Is there a commitment to lifelong learning?

Nineteen-ninety-six was the European Year of Lifelong Learning. It was discussed and celebrated at conference after conference and in a welter of reports. Both the Conservative government and New Labour argued it was essential to create a culture of lifelong learning. This was reinforced by the future Prime Minister Tony Blair, in a declaration the same year that his policies for Britain were: 'education, education and education'. Was the heavy emphasis that Basildonians placed on education evidence that this new political theme had popular resonance? Not quite. Certainly at the time of our survey, a year later, the concept of lifelong learning at least, had had no impact locally.

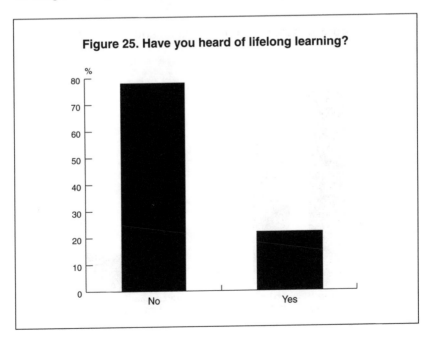

Figure 25. Have you heard of lifelong learning?

Among our respondents 23 per cent claimed to have heard of the phrase 'lifelong learning' and when asked to specify what it meant most referred to past experience or said they didn't have a clue (Figure 25). They made comments such as: 'Going back to college' or ' To keep on learning'. Several years on, and with the help of DFEE and other government publicity campaigns, the terminology may by now have become more commonly understood.

What form of education and training do they want?

When asked what form career advancement would take, 44 per cent of those responding suggested college or university; 33 per cent mentioned on-the-job training (44 per cent if we add day-release and evening classes); 5 per cent specified IT training (Figure 26). This is a considerable endorsement of on-the-job training. The low demand for IT training might have something to do with the base of our sample being skilled working class, and therefore already having had the requisite training. Ten per cent of our sample were working as specialists in jobs related to statistical analysis, design or IT. Training related to IT can be

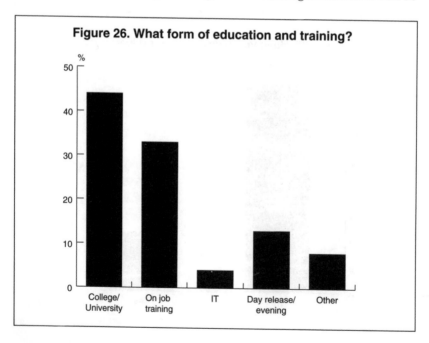

Figure 26. What form of education and training?

seen as part of an 'upskilling' or 'reskilling' trend in the workplace. It certainly has implications for employers and education/training providers because further training will have to be at an advanced level to attract these workers.

There remains a strong commitment to traditional forms of education but there is substantial support for training at work. The former may be evidence of the shift towards the demand for 'soft' skills in the new customer-oriented workplace, while the latter might be considered recognition of the reality of 'credentialism', the need to have a certificate to show that you have the skills to do the job.

What are the policy implications?

The increasing concern with education is not based on anything tangible. We found no strong perception of crumbling and failing schools, of the need for youth training and qualifications for entry to the labour market, nor of the need for 'lifelong learning'. Not a single respondent identified the need for 'basic skills' teaching. In our in-depth interviews, the upgrading of technical, IT or engineering skills was held to be either unnecessary or easily achieved through workplace training. Given the particular nature of our sample of skilled workers, this presents a problem for national and local educational policy-makers, who continue to emphasise literacy, numeracy and employability skills. We do not suggest that these policies are wrong in general, but the majority of Basildonians are already committed to education and therefore these policies have little relevance to them.

The local council's emphasis on the East Basildon Education Action Zone indicates that some, at least, are very much concerned with raising basic educational standards. Education Action Zones aim to be innovative in tackling disadvantage and raising standards through a partnership approach linking schools, council and parents with business, which plays a central role. Local policy-makers hope the EAZ will have an effect in a relatively deprived area of Basildon but early research indicates that zones may bring little in the way of innovation.[19]

There may, however, be one useful achievement if the EAZ brings about a re-alignment of professionals with an interest in improving educational provision. Basildonians, as we will show below are critical of teachers' attitudes, and may welcome such change. A minimum requirement for this would be a willingness by teachers to address the criticisms positively. Whatever the result, it seems that Basildon's EAZ is an appropriate initiative for the particular locality. Our point here is that the locality is exceptional rather than typical of Basildon. To win general support, policy must meet general aspirations, such as the need for more committed teachers.

If it is not EAZs that Basildonians need, what other light can we shed on their concern about education? We can rule out bricks and mortar: more spending on school buildings, equipment and more teachers would not necessarily remove the concern. Our evidence for this is mostly negative. Information from the teachers we talked to, from our visits to schools and to Basildon College did not give us the impression of a decaying and under-resourced educational environment. Like the town, the schools are relatively new, even if their architecture is unfashionable. Our respondents spoke in very specific terms about the state of houses, shops and roads. They did not mention any specific educational needs beyond their criticism of the failures of teachers as a group.

This appears to be a concern across the generations and may have something to do with the difficulties of attracting good teachers to the area. Here is one fairly typical assessment of teachers:

'They're not properly educated. They don't know anything. Especially those that come to Basildon. They despise the kids. They say things like "What can you expect from the kids from round here!" It's not the kids that are the problem, it's the teachers.'

Another respondent told us: 'They will live anywhere but Basildon'. Good teachers and positive experiences were the exception among our respondents.

People clearly want improvements in teachers' attitudes and in their social and educational assumptions. This implies a shift away from the overriding concern with youth training and basic skills programmes, towards a broader educational perspective.

There is some evidence for this in the Basildonian experience of employee assistance programmes (EAPs). When these began in the

1970s in the US they aimed to tackle alcohol and drug-related problems. They soon expanded into a wide range of programmes aimed at tackling personal problems that were not related to work. They 'focussed on the individual, emphasising the importance of physical and mental fitness and the improvement of personal lifestyles'.[20] By the time such a programme was implemented by an international company in Basildon, there was a focus on educational improvement.

The success of the Ford Employee Development and Assistance Programme (EDAP) is instructive. Launched in 1989 Ford's local management expected that 5 per cent of employees would take up a grant to study a non-vocational course. As one adult education teacher who was associated with the scheme told us:

'The take-up came as a surprise as almost a third of the workforce applied for grants. Ford workers were cynical about this as part of their employment package but took the opportunity because it was about personal development, about education. They could study what they liked as long as it was not work-related. This changed later on. It had a great impact on the local colleges and on adult education.'

This scheme soon became directed towards meeting basic skill needs and achieving target numbers of training qualifications. This experience demonstrates the latent demand for education among the workforce: managers were taken aback by the willingness of large numbers of employees to take advantage of the programme.

The real policy challenge would be to give practical effect to the desire of Basildonians for that college course or degree. What that means may be no more than a re-packaging of a liberal education.

Our sample of skilled workers are, by definition, trained and educated beyond a basic level. This means that policy solutions must reflect a higher level of educational need. The issue is not one of *meeting* complex needs but of *determining* those needs.

The EDAP initiative suggests that a direct grant to adults would encourage immediate participation in a new liberal education, although the absence of a grant would not preclude it. A university annex in the town might encourage participation. Such innovations are happening elsewhere. policy-makers might like to consider these options. But our knowledge of Basildonians tells us that they will, in any event, make their own choices about their education.

Linking people and policy-makers

Perhaps the toughest challenge for policy-makers we gathered from our study, is opening new channels of communication with the people of Basildon. The experience of Thatcherism in the eighties may have sounded the death knell for older post-war collective and welfare strategies, but it failed to replace them with anything else. Instead the political style of the populist right succeeded in accelerating a crisis of policy-making and, in particular, further disengaged the population from the framework of local government activity.

Basildon has no representative community institutions. Consultation is generally directed at a narrow and self-appointed layer of the population. And this does represent a change from the past. Representative community institutions did exist – the church, the unions, perhaps the council itself – which spoke for their congregation, membership or constituency. It may still have been an activist minority who had their say, but at least they spoke through legitimate organisations which could mediate the relationship between policy-making institutions and the wider community.

This was a much more active set of relationships than contemporary volunteering or charity giving. Recent work by the Rowntree Foundation has highlighted the gap in voluntary work that used to be part of the role of the shop steward or lay church person.

We are left with characteristically top-down policy-making, devoid of any sense of community involvement or social partnership. Citizens experience it as just another encounter with bureaucracy.

The church was not 'accountable' to its members, but it carried legitimacy and authority by virtue of people's belief in it. The accountability of the unions may have been deeply flawed, but these bodies did command considerable active consent among their memberships.

There is no comparable institution today. What are left are mere shells or their former selves. They are no longer institutions of any significance. The council officers, for all their willingness to consult community groups and set up focus groups, are painfully aware of the limits

Interview with policy-makers 2

'We're trying to readdress that [finding out what people think]. We've commissioned an NOP survey – detailed interviews with 700 residents, which are happening as we speak, which will get a lot of detailed information about quality of life issues, not just about are you happy with the way your bins are emptied. We're not asking those questions, we're asking more what key concerns you have living in Basildon. whether it's the local environment or health or education or whatever. That will feed into and perhaps help to redefine some of the issues we have identified already. We are also consulting all the representative community groups and everything else as well.'

Q. Do they represent anything though?

'This is partly the problem. This is partly why we are going directly to do a public opinion survey. Otherwise you tend to get the usual suspects consulted time and time again. We are going as broadly as we possibly can to as many organisations as we've got. We have found for example that all different parts of this organisation are consulting people all the time and they've all got their own separate consultation lists. We've been doing a huge job to pull the whole lot into one. And then to say, categorise it all, and then to say, well you know let's take a representative snapshot of all of them.

'NOP have done a completely random residents' survey, door to door, in people's homes. Fairly detailed 30-minute interviews. That's what's happening at the moment and that will be 800 or so people.'

Q. That 's going to be a representative cross section?

'Yes. With attention to geographical area because there are big differences in people's views depending on whether they live in Billericay, Wickford – even in parts of the New Town it can vary quite a lot.'

Q. Is that your biggest problem then, or am I just inventing it … to get that public interface and feedback or is there a bigger problem. What is the biggest problem? (See below)

'The biggest problem that the council has…. and the real big challenge … is delivering. Many of these things that we're identifying cannot obviously be achieved by ourselves working in isolation. We have to work in partnership with many different organisations and … you know that if you tell people, we have to really work closely with other partners to deliver. Of course they all have their own agendas. They all have their own plans, their own resource limitations. Trying to bring these organisations together is going to be really difficult.

continued over

'It's starting to happen with, for example, the police. We're merging and having common data bases and common information sources and all of this sort of thing. But in other areas we haven't touched it. For example, in respect of social services and parts of Essex County Council, there are areas where we haven't really got to grips with partnership working. We are trying to be a community leader, and to be a leader people have got to follow you. How do you know what the people out there want? Hence we really have got to know what they want.'

Q. What's the best mechanism for finding out what they want? Is that the problem, finding out what the best mechanism is?

'Partly.... We use loads of mechanisms. You can't use one. In the big survey we're doing with NOP, we ask: would you like to form part of a further consultation? This could be a form of citizens' panel or focus group or whatever; you use a combination of approaches don't you?

'We have conferences on all sorts of specific issues throughout the year. Other people have more formal types of consultation on, say, the local plan. There's more informal consultation. The role of councillors has got to develop, and be more closely aligned with their community so that they're feeding more into the council about what their communities are concerned about. What happens is that councillors come through the door of the council chamber, close it, and never talk to their communities again. He says they start off saying: we represent the community to the council; but what happens is that they end up representing the council to the community.'

of their reach. The groups that do exist are not representative of powerful interest groups or sentiments that are pervasive in society. The very concept of an interest group is frowned upon; Basildonians do not want to be associated with such 'groups'. The perennially consulted are not seen as representative but as individuals with either an axe to grind or nothing better to do with their time.

In the past the active citizen represented a view, however contested, which led and articulated opinion so that it came to be more widely held in the community. Today the community activist represents only themself.

How can the community become involved in democratic decision-making, when the traditional mediating institutions, from the churches to the trade unions to political parties and other civic bodies, no longer play this role?

Community participation and joined-up thinking

Council officers have found themselves caught in a dilemma: how to build community participation into their policy-making when there is such a paucity of community institutions through which to solicit opinions? Yet if they go ahead and take decisions without consultation how can they win legitimacy and trust for those initiatives?

This tension became apparent in a discussion about environmental issues and decision-making (See box over).

During most of this discussion it seems as though the problem is administrative. Only at the end does the possibility of a political resolution occur. This is bound to cause problems. As we reported earlier (pages 46-47), our respondents use 'the environment' to talk about more roads, more car parks, more facilities (including parks and green spaces) and better housing. This is not what policy-makers understand by environmental issues.

The council may well be able to solve its internal conflict through 'joined-up' thinking, developing rational cross-departmental solutions. But this does little to resolve the external conflict, in which, because terms of debate have not even been defined, the council is talking one language while its citizens talk another.

The tension arises because there is no forum in which the administrative efficiency of the council can be tested against the democratic voice of the community. In the old system the political apparatus envisaged policy-making and its execution as a field of struggle. Interests were fought over and one side won. Judgement was made through voting.

The new political framework assumes not political conflict but a consensual model of decision making. But it will not achieve legitimacy if it operates merely to harmonise administrative and technical tensions.

Through partnerships, the council is anxious to link up its policy-making with other policy-oriented agencies and interest groups. This makes sense. But how does this relate to democratic participation?

Our worry is that 'joined-up thinking' may mean nothing more than rational administration of executive policy, which will leave untouched the substantive problem of public involvement.

Let us give one example of what we mean. During our discussions we noted that council officers would often refer to a 'dependency culture'

Interview with policy-makers 3

Yes, clearly there is a trade off between different issues... We've got an example of a direct conflict of policy within the council on a particular issue around the environment: water. The cost of water and the conservation of water. In our Agenda 21 policy it says we should be encouraging everyone to move across to metered water supply. But in the housing strategy we oppose the introduction of water meters into council houses because it will increase people's bills and it has an effect on local deprivation. So you've got two conflicting strands here: one about anti-poverty and one about trying to conserve and enhance the environment.

Q. How will that work itself through the council's chain of command, how will it be debated out?

At the moment it hasn't been debated out and there's a conflict. I think people are starting to recognise that we have got a problem. We've got a multitude of strategies in different areas and the Community Plan is trying to be the over-arching one. And these issues and conflicts are starting to appear. Until recently nobody sat down and said well are these strategies complementary or are certain aspects of them working against each other? That's started to happen — what you might call joined-up thinking. You know, you say: hang on a minute, we've got a conflict her and we should do something about it. How it will be resolved I don't know, to be honest. Probably at the political level.

---

in Basildon. We were troubled by this formulation, not least because it did not fit with our survey results, which affirmed the aspirational tendencies among Basildonians. But the phrase was not being used in the 1980s sense of an underclass, created and sustained by welfare provision.

Council officers were in fact expressing frustration : 'they don't like us, but they keep asking for services'. This is the result of effective participatory forums being absent.

In the perception of Basildonians, 'joined up thinking' may be another exercise in bureaucracy rather than a stimulus to better provision. For all the impact of the eighties the people of Basildon are still the product of the post-war boom, the welfare consensus and the hopes carried into the new town. The inadequacy of services does not lead them to conclude that they should be done away with altogether.

At the moment the council is still perceived as part of the problem. 'Joined up thinking' joins up the council's concerns in a way that makes sense to the council, not in a way that makes sense to Basildonians.

7. Conclusion

Our survey of Basildon has revealed a group of people with some confidence in their ability to make something of their own lives, but with a profound sense that this has to be done in a social, economic and institutional environment which is indifferent or hostile to their hopes and needs.

We suggest that this makes Basildon representative of the experience of living in Britain today. This experience falls between the rhetoric of the metropolitan elites, many of whom talk about 'transforming' society without clearly understanding what most of society is really like, and the systematic exclusion and poverty of the most disadvantaged in Britain. Basildon is representative of those whose life potential was envisioned in the project of post war renewal and reconstruction. It was a social outlook which retained support for between 30 and 40 years. For Basildonians the alliance between state provision and their own aspirations was eroded by the inability of the state to provide effectively in the 1970s and beyond.

The call to get on their bikes was one that many Basildonians had already responded to. It got them to Basildon in the first place. But for most Basildonians, and for millions more throughout Britain in the eighties, getting on in the jungle of the free market was not an equal struggle for the survival of the fittest, but an illustration of privilege and affluence going to those who started off in positions of advantage. The disillusion with bureaucratic inefficiency was replaced by disdain for the self – serving sleaze that surfaced in all areas of public life. The Thatcherite second way had a life span of less than twenty years.

Every indication suggests that the 'Third Way' is even more fragile than its predecessors. New Labour suffers from the bankruptcy of trust in and commitment to public institutions. But its language of delivery and joining up does not resonate with Basildonians, and its emphasis in modernisation has so far done little to create new forms of dialogue and attachment between citizens and public institutions.

This fragility is the latest manifestation of the distance which Basildonians feel from government, political parties and most forms of collective institution. All the evidence of our survey suggests a disengagement from the political sphere and perhaps more importantly from all the intermediary and mediating institutions though which public discussions about priorities used to be conducted. There is no going back to the old institutions. But it is equally artificial to suppose that they can be invented or declared from above.

Basildonians are not prepared to accept the external imposition of priorities. Such priorities cannot be established without a shared framework for public decision making, in which the performance of public services is contextualised. This presumes not only a community of some kind, but the ability to handle and accept conflict.

This brings New Labour's ambition to re-legitimise public services and community life into sharp focus. Without finding new ways to engage the latent social and public concerns of these people, better, more efficient delivery of public services is unlikely to make much different to the quality of their lives.

The effort to create 'joined up government', when set against these challenges, begins to look as if it is creating its own new danger. If joining up just means better integrated, more sophisticated packages of public service delivery, it runs the risk of becoming the solution of a bureaucratic elite. What is needed to make it work for the people of Basildon is for it to be connected to forms of local engagement which build trust and strengthen social capital.

One starting point for this process may be in the deep common concern which most Basildonians hold for education. Another may be a new debate over what the local 'environment' really means, and how it might be improved.

In any case, there is a clear implication from this local analysis: Thatcherism has both failed and succeeded, and its success has made it more difficult for any form of public or collective enterprise to win the legitimacy it surely needs. As more and more are beginning to recognise, it may be the most important seeds of solutions to this crisis of the state lie, not in government itself, but in a new approach to the institutions of civil society.

Appendix 1. Basildon MPs since 1945

Year	MP	Party	Majority over nearest rival
1945 (Boundary change)	Ray Gunter	(Lab)	3,591
1950/51	Bernard Braine	(Con)	4,366 /6,323
1955 (Boundary change Billericay constituency)	Richard Body	(Con)	4,206 First election result reported
1959	Edward Gardner	(Con)	4,822 First election result in a record tine of 59 minutes
1964	Edward Gardner	(Con)	1,592
1966	Eric Moonman	(Lab)	1,642
1970	Robert McCrindle	(Con)	3,954
1974/74 (Boundary change Basildon constituency)	Eric Moonman	(Lab)	11,000 /10,551 Labour Council & Constituency
1979	Harvey Proctor	(Con)	5,180
1983 (Boundary change)	David Amess	(Con)	1,379 Proctor moved to a safe seat in Billericay
1987	David Amess	(Con)	2,649 Teresa Gorman elected for Billericay
1992	David Amess	(Con)	1, 480
1997	Angela Smith	(New Lab)	13,280

Notes

1. See Appendix 1. Lucas P, 1991, *Basildon*, Phillimore, Chichester, is a readable introduction to the history of the new town. See also Osborn FJ and Whittick A, 1997, *New Towns, Their Origins, Achievements and Progress*, Hill, London, ch20, pp205-219 and, for statistics, Evans H, 1972, *New Towns: The British Experience*, Town and country Planning Association/Charles King, London, pp173-189.

2. Hayes D & Hudson A, 2001, *Who are the C2s? A Social and Political Attitudes Survey, Basildon, 1992*, reprinted with a new introduction: *Basildon Revisited: Change and Continuity*, E&WRG, Whitstable.

3. 'MP Fumes at Minister's Essex Man Slur', *Thurrock Gazette*, 1 January 1993.

4. Hayes & Hudson, 2001, op cit, Appendix II.

5. Basildon's population was 161,124 in 1991 and rose to just under 163,000 in 1996. Predictions are that it will reach 168,000 by 2011. Of this 80,829 are economically active. Of this group light manufacturing, craft and technical workers constitute 48 per cent of the male working population, 4 per cent higher than the national average. 37 per cent of the female workforce is predominantly occupied in clerical or secretarial work, 8 per cent higher than the national average. This is in line with the shift to service work in the area. (Figures adapted from Policy Unit, 1997 and 1998, *Basildon Trends and Basildon Trends Supplement*, Basildon District Council).

6. Quoted in Greenslade R, 1992, 'Up the Workers', *The Times*, 27 June 1992.

7 Lucas, 1991, op cit, p56.

8. *Basildon Standard*, 1963, quoted in Lucas, 1991, op cit, p56.

9. Speaking at a public meeting in Laindon on 7 October 1948. When this speech was recalled by Council Leader John Potter on the fiftieth anniversary of the designation of the new town, the sentence about ugliness and grime was omitted ('Signing up to celebrate 50 years of the new town', *District Diary*, Spring 1999, p30).

10. Adonis A and Pollard S, 1998, *A Class Act: The myth of Britain's classless society*, Penguin, London, p7.

11. Adonis and Pollard, 1998, ibid, p10.

12. Bentley T, Jupp B and Stedman-Jones D, 2000, *Getting to grips with depoliticisation*, Demos, London, p7.

13. See Willkinson H, ed, 2000, *Family Business*, Demos, London.

14. Policy Unit, 1997, *Basildon Trends*, Basildon District Council, Basildon, p6.

15. Bentley, Jupp and Stedman-Jones, 2000, op cit, pp14-16.

16. Hudson A, Hayes D and Andrew T, 1996, *Working Lives in the 1990s: Preliminary findings of the Attitudes to Work Survey*, Global Futures, London, s.4.1. See also Hayes D and Hudson A, 2001 (forthcoming), *Attitudes to Work*, E&WRG.

17. Hudson, Hayes and Andrew, 1996, op cit. See also Hayes and Hudson, 2001 (forthcoming), op cit.

18. Goldthorpe JH, Lockwood D, Bechhoffer F and Plant J, 1968, *The Affluent Worker: Industrial attitudes and behaviour*, Cambridge University Press, Cambridge, pp128-130.

19. Pye D, 1999, 'What Goes Around